Spiritual Inclination

Severine Bateman

BookLeaf Publishing

India | USA | UK

Presentation by *BookLeaf Publishing*

Web: www.bookleafpub.com

E-mail: info@bookleafpub.com

ISBN: 9789360947415

First edition 2024

*I would like to dedicate this book to all
those who believed in me.*

Perspective

Where I look
That is all that really matters

Where I look,
Is where my path will lead

Where I look,
Will dictate my future actions

Where I look,
Will determine what i seek

If I look,
In more than one direction

Im sure my look,
Will be split in more than two

But if I look,
Towards where i may be steady

Than my look,
I'm sure will be turned to you.

Where I Am Led

I feel blind, left behind, and forgotten

I feel lost, left alone, and uncared for

I have felt this way on many occasion

And yet this time, is worse than I have born

Where did I go wrong, where was my mistake?

What road did I miss that has led me here?

How did i stumble i to this forsaken place?

What other burdens am I meant to bear?

And yet, I see these words, all self-pity

A focus put on my evergrowing woes

I can see it, with utmost clarity

I can see how my heart has grown

My burdens may be very many

And quite possibly quite true

But such focus will not brimg harmony

That i will only obtain through You

So may my eyes be turned heavenwards

And may my desirrs be made bright

I shall try to seek yoy every day

And sendmy prayers to you by night.

Remember

I try to remember every day
The mercy that's been shown to me.

I try to seek in every way
The will of whom i strive to be

Sometimes i feel closer
To that standard i wish to bear

Other times I'm farther
Farther than I ever care to share

I want to always remember
He who has allowed me to come

Yet sometimes I seek closure
And feel ive been dragged so far from home

Why must i always struggle
Even when i knowy heart is right

Sometimes life feels like a puzzle
Makimg me feel im not so bright

Yet even when i protest

And demand that i be set free

Im forced to face my weakness
And remember he is best for me

So even if i flounder
And feel the burdens ha e been placed

I know I have a Savior
Who someday i will see His face.

Uncommon

Are we meant to be common
Or should we stand apart

Just like the rest of the world
Or completely different from the start

Should we seek to be like those around us
Or should we walk a differnt path

Do i base my worth on their standards
Or do i fear a greater wrath

The requests from the world are easy
And yet seem muddled along the way

With so many different stanards present
How can i know which to obey

But if I am uncommon
And look to You for the way

I fear Ill be abandoned
And find theres no place for me to stay

Such thoughts, they truly scare me,

Provide a reason for me to pause

And yet, when i take time to think and look
I find security in Your laws

Yes i might be uncommon
And yes I might need to stand apart

But I know that You'll be with me
You have been from the start.

What Seekest Thou

What seekest thou?
What is it that you want?

What serkest thou?
Do you wish to stand avant?

What seekest thou?
What to you has value?

What seekest thou?
Do you want to know what's true?

What seekest thou?
Would you want to heed the call?

What seekest thou?
What makes you stumble and fall?

What seekest thou?
Do you strive to walk alone?

What seekest thou?
What path will lead you home?

What seekest thou?

Whose will do you care to follow?

What seekest thou?
Does your life to you fell hollow?

What seekest thou?
I can tell you what you seek.

What seekest thou?
To Him you aught to speak.

What seekest thou?
There is a kingdom beyond compare.

What seekest thou?
He can safely takr you there.

But what seekest thou?
What is the life you want to live

No matter what you seeketh
His love he freely gives

But what seeketh thou?
He never will force you to go

It depends on what you seeketh
Your desire you must show.

His Suffering

He lies there in utter agony
Secluded in a grove of trees

Sometimes i try to stetch forth my hand
And place it on His within the painting
His clothes are white, just like His soul
And yet it will be dyed red from His sacrifice

I can feel the love He has radiate from the
parchment

Trust

How does one trust Him
When there's no peace to be found
unless there is faith.

Hope Power Faith

So often hope evades me
in a world devoid of care.

Each day I kneel and cry out
to ask if He is there.

When my life lacks all direction
and I feel that hope is lost,

I just turn my eyes toward heaven
and seek you at all costs.

Although this life is heavy
and although the way's unclear,

through Him I hope for tomorrow
that He'll lead me safely there.

How Will I live

13

How will I live,
what will I choose?
How will I focus
my life's pursuit?

What will I choose,
how will I act?
My life's pursuit,
what are the facts?

How will I act
when life is hard?
What are the facts,
will I stay on guard?

When life is hard,
I won't back down.
I will stay on guard,
He can be found.

Peace

How may Peace be found?
My peace is but a moment,
but His, eternal.

The Choice

There is a choice laid before you,
a decision that you must make.

The options lead down two paths,
you must decide which to take.

The first will lead to glory,
to admiration from your peers.

The second is more humble,
more costly, filled with tears.

The first is filled with riches,
and more fruit than you can eat.

The second will be filled with hunger,
and no cover for your feet.

The first, it may feel empty,
but there will be friends around.

The second holds betrayal,
no support as you hit the ground.

The first path, it is desired,
most would find a better trip.

Yet the second seems to call you,
you're enamored by the script.

While the first is full of glory
and the envy of mankind,

the second holds more meaning,
filled with treasures for you to find.

So while the world may seek the first path,
and coerce you to do the same,

I know my Savior walked the second,
and I wish to follow in His name.

Respite

Sometimes I wonder where I should turn for
care
in a world that seems to be oh so busy.
I cannot seem to feel whether He is there.
When did my burdens start to grow so heavy.

And yet I feel that I must hold on tightly,
and seek more strength, from Him and those
around me.
When I turn to Him and can forget my woes
and seek more healing from my many sorrows.

He lives

He lives
and He guides me.
He reaches out to me.
He will always love me, and I
just trust.

One Day At A Time

One day at a time.
That's how life happens.
There is no fast pass
to make it fly by.

One step forward.
That's how you begin.
You will go nowhere
if you do not even start.

One step forward.
That's all it takes.
To change life's direction
and become who you know you can be.

One day at a time.
Your life will change slowly.
You just may be surprised
by what you are capable of.

A Mustard Seed

To really change can take great effort.
The change perhaps slow to be seen.
But you can change with desire.
You can let the past go.
You can start anew.
If you will have
but the faith
of a
seed.

Waiting

21

Sometimes I feel I am left to wait,
stranded on a far away shore.
Ifeel that I am before a gate,
locked and buried evermore,
truly abandoned to the core.

Yet a voice seems to call to me,
and leads me through the door.
I will not be left here easily.
It shows me what I'm meant to be.

Peace and Love

22

Peace can be hard to find.
Each day can be a struggle.
And obstacles are in the way,
Center stage in your life
Even though you'd wish to avoid them.

Ample time is likely wasted in
Needing answers that can't be found,
Despite great and ceaseless effort.

Longing for the meaning
Of the life you are leading
Very well may be
Evident in what you're reading.

Striving

I wish I could strive
to seek You and life's meaning.
Yet I find myself
every day in struggling
to go meet you where you stand.

What Do I seek

24

I don't know
what I wish to know
about life,
about love,
about what it is I seek
when I'm on my own.

Yet I know
what I want to want
in this life,
for all time,
is to know what I seek
in the world above.

Today

Today.

Stressful, dreadful,

demanding, overbearing, tiring,

bright morning, dark night,

promising, anticipating, liking,

excited, prepared,

Tomorrow

Fortune Favors The Bold

Remember, fortune favors the bold.
You can control your life, go fight and win.
A miracle you just might behold.

Do not let your beating heart grow cold.
Just harness the burning fire within.
Remember, fortune favors the bold.

The path ahead may be laid with gold.
So, hold on, stay the course my dear friend.
A miracle you just might behold.

Do not let your story go untold.
There is history upon your skin.
Remember, fortune favors the bold.

A life well written cannot be sold.
So, strive to live your best life herein.
A miracle you just might behold.

Through your efforts greatness will unfold.
You need not wonder what might have been.
Remember, fortune favors the bold.
A miracle you just might behold.